Aces of aviation

From 1914 to the present

Phillips Tahuer

Ediciones Afrodita

Contents

Introduction

• Korean War (1950-1953)

1. Nikolai Sutyagin (Soviet Union) – 22 kills in jet aircraft.
2. Yevgeny Pepelyaev (Soviet Union) – 23 kills.
3. James Jabara (US) – First American jet ace, 15 kills.
4. Joseph McConnell (US) – 16 kills in the Korean War.

• Vietnam War (1955-1975)

1. Nguyễn Văn Cốc (North Vietnam) – 9 confirmed and up to 13 claimed kills.
2. Charles B. DeBellevue (US) – 6 kills.
3. Jeffrey Feinstein (US) – 5 kills, becoming one of the last American aces.

• Later Conflicts

1. Giora Epstein (Israel) – With 17 kills, the most victorious jet fighter ace in the world, active in the Arab-Israeli Wars.
2. Yiftah Spector (Israel) – 15 victories
3. Majid Zugbi (Syria) – 6 confirmed victories in the Arab-Israeli wars.

Introduction

Since the birth of aerial combat in World War I, the term "ace" has resonated strongly in military history, describing those pilots with an exceptional talent for maneuvering and winning in the skies. Being an "ace" not only represented having shot down five or more enemy aircraft, but was a symbol of skill, bravery, and mastery in one of the most complex and lethal disciplines of modern warfare. Over time, aerial combat has evolved significantly, and with it, the profile of the aces who have marked each conflict. From the fabric and wood planes of 1914 to the advanced fighter jets of today, the "ace" continues to be an admired figure, and their stories, are a display of skill in life-or-death situations.

In this book, we will explore the biographies of the most important aces of each war, from the pioneers of World War I to the pilots of contemporary wars. We will meet legendary figures such as the Red Baron, Manfred von Richthofen, and the ace with the most kills in history, Erich Hartmann, who stood out in their respective historical moments. Each biography will not only detail achievements and confrontations but will also put into context the evolution of combat aviation and how each conflict shaped new strategies and skills in the art of aerial warfare.

"Ace of Aviation" is, thus, a journey through the history of war seen from above, where the protagonists are men and women who flew with courage and skill, facing challenges both technical and human. Through their biographies, we will discover how the concept of "ace" has endured and adapted over time, remembering their legacies in the skies from 1914 to the present day.

We must clarify that, in modern conflicts, such as the wars in Iraq, Afghanistan, and other regions, aerial confrontations are less frequent due to advances in technology and the use of drones. The structure of air combat has changed, and the traditional concept of a "fighter ace" is less common today.

Below is a list of pilots considered to be the greatest "aviation aces" from World War I to the present, who achieved a significant number of kills in air combat and stood out for their skills and bravery.

World War I (1914-1918)

The First World War marked the debut of military aviation as a decisive factor in armed conflict, a transformation that left an indelible mark on the course of the war and the history of aviation. At the start of the war, aircraft were simple reconnaissance machines, used primarily to observe enemy positions and report troop movements. However, as countries realized their strategic potential, the role of aviation rapidly evolved, moving from observation to defense and attack.

The first aerial encounters between rival pilots were almost chivalrous, exchanging salutes or pistol shots. Soon, however, fixed machine guns synchronized with the propellers were adopted, giving rise to the first aerial combats or "dogfights." Thus arose the concept of the "ace" of aviation, an honorary title awarded to those pilots who achieved five or more kills, and which filled the skies with legends such as the Red Baron, Manfred von Richthofen, who shot down 80 enemy aircraft and became an icon of aerial warfare.

The war in the air intensified with the use of bombers, such as the Zeppelin and the German Gotha bombers, which took the war directly to the cities, sowing fear and opening a new front of psychological warfare. Aircraft also played a key role in field artillery, directing fire through air communication and providing precision in ground attacks.

Towards the end of the war, aviation changed the way of thinking about war conflicts. World War I demonstrated the strategic and tactical value of aviation, laying the groundwork for the development of specialized air forces and the essential role of aircraft in future conflicts. Although airplanes were primitive compared to today's, their impact on warfare was profound, transforming aviation into a fundamental pillar of modern warfare.

Among the greatest aces of the conflict were:

1. Manfred von Richthofen: "The Red Baron"

Manfred von Richthofen, known as "The Red Baron," is one of history's most legendary fighter pilots and the most renowned flying ace of World War I. He was born on May 2, 1892, in Breslau, Germany (now Wrocław, Poland), to a Prussian noble family, and grew up in an aristocratic environment, with training in horse riding, hunting, and sports. From an early age, Richthofen displayed a strong competitive spirit and a penchant for adventure, qualities that would accompany him in his career as a pilot.

Richthofen began his military life in the German cavalry, but with the development of trench warfare in World War I, the cavalry lost relevance. Seeking new challenges, Richthofen requested a transfer to the Air Force, where he initially served as an observer. Under the influence of Oswald Boelcke, a pioneer of aerial combat tactics and an experienced pilot, Richthofen trained as a fighter pilot and began his career in the skies.

In 1916, Manfred von Richthofen made his first confirmed kill, and from that moment on his skill and precision earned him unparalleled prestige. He quickly distinguished himself by painting his aircraft, an Albatros D.III and later a Fokker Dr.I triplane, bright red, a bold choice that made him easily identifiable in the sky and earned him the nickname "The Red Baron." Richthofen developed a combat style that prioritized precision, control, and discipline, which allowed him to achieve 80 confirmed kills, the highest number in World War I.

During his career, he led the "Jagdgeschwader 1," also known as the "Flying Circus," an elite squadron of pilots who, like him, painted their planes in bright colors. The Flying Circus, which was highly respected and feared, had a psychological impact on the enemy. Richthofen and his squadron's planes were not only lethal, but they symbolized the German air threat to the Allies.

Richthofen was killed in combat on April 21, 1918, at the age of 25, after being shot while chasing an enemy plane over the Somme River in France. Although theories persist to this day about who was responsible for his death (either anti-aircraft fire from the ground or Canadian pilot Roy Brown), his downing marked a crucial moment in the history of the war. The Allies paid tribute to him at his funeral, recognizing his skill, bravery, and ethics as a pilot.

Manfred von Richthofen, "The Red Baron," went on to command 58 missions in which he shot down 80 confirmed aircraft, a record that could not be surpassed in the First World War. By the end of the war, her flying squadron had shot down 644 aircraft and suffered only 56 casualties, for which she was awarded the Cross of Merit. Richthofen remains one of the most studied and admired figures in military aviation, and her legacy lives on as a symbol of skill and chivalry in aerial combat. Her impact not only defined combat standards in her time but also immortalized the concept of the "ace" in aviation.

2. René Fonck: The French Ace of World War I

René Fonck, considered one of the most prominent aviation aces of World War I, was born on March 27, 1894, in the city of Verdun, France. From a young age, he showed a strong interest in aviation and mechanics, which led him to enter the military world and, later, to become a pilot. At the outbreak of World War I in 1914, Fonck joined the French Army, where he initially served in the artillery before transferring to aviation in 1915.

Fonck received his pilot's license and began flying as an observer in reconnaissance aircraft. However, he soon realized that his true passion was aerial combat, which led him to become a fighter pilot. In 1916, he joined the 103rd Fighter Squadron, where he began his career as a flying ace. His skill in the air and accuracy with weapons soon earned him recognition, and he quickly stood out among his peers.

As the war progressed, Fonck honed his combat style, characterized by its methodical and tactical approach. He is credited with a total of 75 confirmed kills, making him the most successful French fighter ace of the war and one of the greatest in history. His record earned him numerous decorations, including the Cross of the Legion of Honour, the Military Medal, and several other distinctions.

Fonck was not only known for his skill as a pilot but also his charismatic personality and approach to war. He became a national hero in France, and his image was used to promote the war effort. In 1917, he was appointed leader of the 103rd Fighter Squadron, where he continued to inspire his fellow pilots and improve air combat tactics.

Despite his success in the air, war was a constant challenge. Fonck survived multiple engagements and escaped dangerous situations, but he also experienced the loss of friends and comrades in combat. His determination and exceptional skills led him to become a legendary figure in aviation history.

By the end of the war in 1918, René Fonck was considered a war hero in France and received international recognition for his achievements. After the war, he continued to be involved in aviation, working on the development of new aircraft and participating in various air competitions. He also had a brief stint in politics and the aeronautical industry in the following decades.

Fonck died on June 18, 1953, in New York, United States, but his legacy as one of the greatest flying aces and a pioneer of aerial combat lives on. His bravery, skill, and contributions to aviation during World War I continue to be remembered and celebrated, making him a symbol of military aviation and a hero in French history.

3. Billy Bishop: The Canadian Ace of World War I

William Avery "Billy" Bishop was born on February 8, 1894, in Owen Sound, Ontario, Canada. From a young age, he showed a strong interest in aviation and an adventurous spirit that led him to join the Canadian armed forces at the outbreak of World War I in 1914. Initially, he served in the infantry, but his desire to fly led him to request a transfer to the British Royal Flying Corps (RFC).

Bishop received his pilot training in 1916, and after completing his training, he was assigned to the RFC's 60 Squadron in France. He quickly proved himself to be a talented and daring pilot. His first confirmed kill came in June 1917, and he soon gained a reputation as one of the war's finest fighters. His bold and aggressive approach to aerial combat, coupled with his tactical skill, allowed him to rack up victories in the air quickly and effectively.

Throughout his flying career, Billy Bishop became one of the most successful aces of World War I, achieving a total of 72 confirmed kills. This feat made him the second most decorated flying ace of the war, after Germany's Manfred von Richthofen. Bishop was awarded the Victoria Cross, Britain's highest military decoration, for his bravery and exceptional skills in combat.

One of Bishop's most notable actions took place on June 2, 1917, when, on a solo mission, he made a daring raid on a German airfield. On this mission, he shot down several enemy aircraft and destroyed others on the ground. This heroic act was instrumental in cementing his status as a war hero in Canada and the British Empire.

Bishop also played a major role in developing air combat tactics and improving pilot training. In 1918, he was appointed commander of the 85th Squadron, where he continued to lead other pilots in aerial combat. By the end of the war, he had achieved celebrity status, not only in Canada but also in the aviation world.

After the war, Bishop continued his career in civil aviation and became involved in various business activities. He became an advocate for aviation and worked to promote the aircraft industry in Canada. He was also a member of the Canadian Parliament and took an interest in the development of military aviation in his country.

Billy Bishop died on 11 September 1956 in the state of Florida, USA, but his legacy lives on. His bravery, skill, and contributions to air combat and Canadian aviation have made him an iconic figure in military history. His life and achievements are remembered and celebrated, and his name remains synonymous with heroism and excellence in aviation.

4. Ernst Udet: A Legendary German Flying Ace

Ernst Udet was born on April 26, 1896, in Freiburg, Germany. From a young age, he showed a remarkable interest in aviation and mechanics, which led him to join the German army in 1914 at the outbreak of World

War I. He initially served in the infantry, but soon moved into aviation, where he became a pilot.

Udet received his pilot training in 1916 and was assigned to the Jasta 37 fighter squadron, where he began his career as a flying ace. His first victory in aerial combat came in 1917, and he quickly stood out for his bravery and exceptional skills in the air. As he racked up victories, Udet became one of the most prominent pilots of the conflict, achieving a total of 62 confirmed kills. His combat style was bold and aggressive, making him a feared rival for his opponents.

Ernst Udet gained a reputation for his skill in handling aircraft, especially in his famous Fokker D.VII fighter, which became a symbol of his success in combat. Not only was Udet an excellent pilot, but he was also known for his charismatic personality and love of adventure. He was often seen taking part in aerobatics and demonstrations, which increased his popularity and made him a national hero in Germany.

Throughout the war, Udet received numerous decorations for his achievements, including the Iron Cross's first and second class. His success in aerial combat led to him being one of the most decorated aces of the war, alongside other legendary pilots such as Manfred von Richthofen and René Fonck.

Following the end of World War I in 1918, Udet faced a new challenge: the transition from military to civilian life. Despite economic hardship and political instability in Germany, he continued to be involved in aviation. He worked as a test pilot and performed aerobatics for various exhibitions, where he displayed his mastery of the air.

In the 1920s, Udet became an advocate of aviation and worked to promote the development of the aircraft industry in Germany. He was a fervent proponent of the country's air rearmament in the 1930s, and his knowledge and experience led to his holding various positions in the Luftwaffe, the German air force, following the Nazi regime's rise to power.

However, Udet's life took a dark turn. As World War II intensified, Udet found himself under increasing pressure and at odds with the policies of the Luftwaffe high command. In November 1941, unable to bear the stress and frustration, Ernst Udet took his own life, a tragic end for a man who had been a symbol of bravery and skill in aviation.

Ernst Udet left a legacy in the history of military aviation. His skill as a pilot, his contribution to air tactics, and his charismatic personality made him an iconic figure in the history of World War I. His life and career continue to be remembered and studied as a testament to the courage and complexity of wartime aviation.

5. Edward "Mick" Mannock: A Brave British Flying Ace

Edward Mannock, known as "Mick," was born on May 24, 1887, in the Finsbury neighborhood of London, United Kingdom. Coming from a family of Irish origin, he grew up in an environment that pushed him toward a life of adventure and challenge. Before World War I, he worked in a variety of occupations, including as an electrical engineer and in the railroad industry, where he developed technical skills that would later prove useful to him as a pilot.

At the outbreak of World War I, Mannock enlisted in the British Army, initially serving in the Corps of Royal Engineers. However, his desire to fly led him to apply for a transfer to the Royal Flying Corps (RFC) in 1916. After completing his pilot training, he was assigned to No. 40 Squadron, where he began his career in aerial combat.

Mick Mannock quickly distinguished himself as a daring and talented pilot. Throughout his career, he managed to shoot down 61 enemy aircraft, becoming one of the most successful aces of World War I. His innovative and tactical approach to air combat, which combined aggressive maneuvering with a methodical approach, helped him excel in the skies of Europe. He was also known for his ability to perform diving attacks, which surprised his opponents and allowed him to shoot down aircraft in unfavorable circumstances.

As his reputation grew, Mannock became a leader in his squadron and a mentor to younger pilots. His charismatic personality and dedication to the welfare of his fellow pilots made him a much-loved figure. In 1917, he was awarded the Distinguished Flying Cross (DFC) for his bravery and achievements in combat, and his status as a national hero was further cemented after he was awarded the Victoria Cross, Britain's highest military honor, for extraordinary bravery in the air.

Mannock was not only a brave fighter, but he also displayed a deep sense of responsibility towards his men. He was known for his concern for the safety of his fellow pilots and his insistence on proper training and preparation before going into combat. His humane approach to aviation made him stand out not only as an exceptional pilot but as an inspiring leader.

Sadly, on July 26, 1918, his career and life came to a tragic end. Mannock was shot down in an aerial combat near the town of Arras, France, and died at the age of 31. His loss was deeply felt by his comrades and by the entire British nation, who had come to see in him a symbol of courage and sacrifice.

Edward "Mick" Mannock left a legacy in the history of military aviation. His bravery, exceptional skills, and leadership have made him an iconic figure of World War I. Today, he is remembered not only for his success in the air but also for his humanity and commitment to his fellow soldiers, making him a true hero of British aviation. His story continues to inspire future generations and is a testament to the courage and camaraderie that characterize fighter pilots.

The role of aviation in the Spanish Civil War

The Spanish Civil War (1936-1939) was the first conflict in which modern aviation played a pivotal role, setting precedents for air warfare in World War II. Both sides, the Republicans and the Nationalists, were supported by foreign powers who provided aircraft, pilots, and tactical expertise. This air conflict not only determined the military advantage of the Nationalists but also served as a testing ground for tactics and technologies that would later be widely used on the global stage.

The Republican side received air support primarily from the Soviet Union, which provided aircraft such as the Polikarpov I-15 and I-16 fighters and Tupolev SB-2 bombers. These aircraft, although effective in combat, faced difficulties against the Nationalist air forces, which had the experience and resources provided by Nazi Germany and Fascist Italy. The Republican aviation included volunteer pilots of different nationalities, organized into the famous International Brigades. Despite their courage and commitment, the Republican pilots lacked the organization, training, and logistical maintenance of the Nationalists, which limited their effectiveness in combat.

The Nationalist side, led by Francisco Franco, had crucial support from Nazi Germany and Fascist Italy, countries that sent entire military units to support the Nationalists. Germany was noted for the creation of the Condor Legion, an elite unit composed of Messerschmitt Bf 109 fighters, Heinkel He 111, and

Junkers Ju 52 bombers, as well as a contingent of experienced German pilots and technicians.

The Condor Legion carried out bombing missions that proved decisive, with the attack on the town of Guernica being one of the most devastating and symbolic episodes of the war. This aerial bombardment, immortalized in a painting by Pablo Picasso, was one of the first to use carpet bombing tactics to destroy civilian targets, a strategy that would become common in World War II.

The Spanish Civil War was a laboratory for aerial warfare tactics, which included strategic bombing, dive attacks, and formation air combat techniques. Nazi Germany, through the Condor Legion, perfected the use of dive bombing with the Junkers Ju 87 Stuka and aerial combat with the Messerschmitt Bf 109, fighters that would later be instrumental in its offensive in Europe.

Italy, for its part, contributed a fleet of Fiat CR.32 aircraft, biplane fighters that were used effectively against the Republican air forces. The use of these fighters, although more outdated compared to monoplanes, demonstrated their effectiveness in close combat and agile maneuvers, sometimes prevailing over the more modern Republican fighters.

In addition to its strategic value, aviation in the Spanish Civil War was a propaganda tool and a symbol of superiority. The aerial bombing of Republican cities, such as Guernica and Madrid, had a profound psychological impact on the civilian population, demonstrating the terror that indiscriminate bombing could inflict. This propaganda aspect strengthened the nationalist narrative, and demoralized Republican forces and their supporters.

Aviation in the Spanish Civil War played a decisive and complex role, both on the battlefield and in the psychology of war. The experience gained in this conflict shaped the way Germany and Italy would employ aviation in World War II, also influencing the air tactics and strategies of other countries. The Spanish Civil War demonstrated the devastating potential of modern air warfare and marked the beginning of an era in which air dominance would become an essential element in large-scale wars.

1. Joaquín García-Morato y Castaño: Spanish aviation ace and hero of the Civil War

Joaquín García-Morato y Castaño was one of the most outstanding pilots of Spanish aviation during the Spanish Civil War (1936-1939) and is recognized as the main aviation ace of the Nationalist side. With 40 confirmed aerial victories, García-Morato left an indelible mark on the history of Spanish military aviation. His skill in aerial combat, his leadership, and his bravery earned him the admiration and respect of both his colleagues and his adversaries.

Joaquín García-Morato was born on May 4, 1904, in Melilla, Spain, to a military family. From a young age, he showed great interest in aviation and decided to join the Aeronautics Military Flight School in Cuatro Vientos, Madrid, in 1925. Throughout his formative years, García-Morato stood out for his skill and discipline, and in a short time, he became an exceptional pilot, being designated a flight instructor.

Before the Civil War, he participated in campaigns in North Africa, where he accumulated experience in flight and military tactics. These years of training and combat would be crucial to the success of his future exploits in the Spanish Civil War.

With the outbreak of the Spanish Civil War in 1936, García-Morato joined the Nationalist side and was assigned to the fighter squadron. Commanding a Fiat CR.32, a biplane fighter supplied by Fascist Italy, García-Morato quickly demonstrated his skills, obtaining his first victories against the Republican forces. Thanks to his combat prowess, he became the leader of the Blue Patrol, an elite unit made up of some of the best pilots on the Nationalist side.

The Blue Patrol took part in key air battles, including the defense of airspace on the Madrid front and the offensive on the Aragon front. García-Morato proved to be a master of maneuvers and close combat, establishing himself as the most feared and respected pilot of the conflict. Throughout the war, his aerial victories and combat leadership made him a central figure in Nationalist propaganda.

Throughout the Civil War, Joaquín García-Morato amassed a total of 40 confirmed aerial victories, becoming the greatest flying ace of the war. His Fiat CR.32 aircraft was particularly agile and effective in close combat, and García-Morato took full advantage of these characteristics when facing Soviet-made

Republican aircraft, such as the Polikarpov I-15 and I-16.

His ability to plan and execute combat missions with precision was legendary, and his leadership allowed him to train other pilots who would become leading figures in Spanish aviation. García-Morato was not only admired for his combat skill but also his respect for the rules of aerial combat, displaying nobility and professionalism in every engagement.

On April 4, 1939, just days after the end of the Civil War, Joaquín García-Morato lost his life in a tragic accident while performing an exhibition flight at the Griñón airfield, Madrid. During an aerobatic maneuver, his plane suffered a failure that cost the Spanish ace his life at the age of 34.

Despite his short life, García-Morato left a legacy in the history of Spanish aviation. He was decorated with numerous medals and honors, including the Laureate Cross of San Fernando, the highest Spanish military distinction. In his honor, several Spanish air patrols and facilities have been named after him. García-Morato became a symbol of courage and skill, and his career inspired generations of fighter pilots in Spain and around the world.

2. Sergei Ivanovich Gritsevets: Soviet flying ace in the Spanish Civil War

Sergei Ivanovich Gritsevets was one of the most prominent pilots in Soviet aviation, known for his exploits in the Spanish Civil War and during the Battle of Khalkhin Gol on the border between Mongolia and Manchuria. Born on 19 July 1909 in the small town of Borovtsy, in what is now Belarus, Gritsevets distinguished himself as an exceptional leader and a skilled pilot, earning the title of Hero of the Soviet Union on two occasions. During his participation in the Spanish Civil War, Gritsevets left a significant mark on the conflict, achieving numerous aerial victories and aiding the Republican cause against Francoist forces.

In 1931 he joined the Red Army, in 1932 he completed his pilot training at the Orenburg Military Academy, and in 1936 he completed his air combat training at the Odessa Pilot School. In the spring of 1938, he voluntarily traveled to China and took part in the fight against the Japanese attack on Wuhan. He scored two or three victories in a 30-minute air fight and shot down 21 Japanese aircraft. Griesevets flew either a Polikarpov I-15 biplane or an I-16 monoplane. That same year, Griesevets also volunteered for the Spanish Civil War in defense of the Second Republic and remained there until the end of 1938, when all Soviet pilots had to return. Flying the I-16, he scored 30 aerial victories over Spain and received his first Hero of the Soviet Union and Gold Star Medal on 22 February 1939. On 29 May 1939, a group of 48 experienced pilots, including Gritsevest, was sent to Mongolia as the backbone of the new air force. There Gritsevest took part in numerous operations against Japanese aircraft. On 26 June, during the Battle of Harkhingor, Gritsevest and his commander, Major V. Zabaluyev, landed the I-16. The latter's engine was damaged, and it had to land 60 meters from the Japanese defense lines. Zabaluyev boarded Gritsevest's plane and they fled together. For this, along with his other actions during the conflict, he received the second title of Hero of the Soviet Union on 29 August of the same year. During this period, Griesevests shot down a total of 11 Japanese aircraft.

On 12 September 1939, Griesevest and 20 other pilots were sent to Ukraine in preparation for the invasion of Poland on 17 September. Griesevest was killed the day before in an accident at Borbasov, near Vitebsk, when the plane collided with him as he prepared to take off. Griesevest shot down a total of 42 enemy aircraft, two of which were biplanes. A monument was erected to him at Baranavič.

Gritsevets was known for his precise and meticulous combat style. He used his knowledge of the performance of Soviet aircraft to maximize their effectiveness on the battlefield, carrying out surprise attacks and risky maneuvers. He was able to hold strategic positions during combat and had a keen ability to anticipate his opponents' movements, allowing him to maintain the upper hand in engagements.

In addition to his skill in aerial combat, Gritsevets also distinguished himself as a leader on the battlefield. He trained his fellow pilots and shared their tactics, which strengthened Republican air units in Spain. His leadership helped increase the effectiveness of

Republican air forces in the fight against Franco's side, and his participation in the conflict established him as one of the best Soviet fighter pilots.

3. Julio Salvador y Díaz-Benjumea: Spanish Aviation Ace in the Spanish Civil War

Julio Salvador y Díaz-Benjumea was one of the top Spanish aviation aces during the Spanish Civil War, fighting on the side of the Nationalist forces. Recognized for his combat prowess and ability to lead squadrons, Salvador y Díaz-Benjumea achieved great fame among his peers and superiors, becoming one of the most respected fighter pilots of his time. During the conflict, he racked up numerous aerial victories and played a key role in consolidating Nationalist aviation as an effective force in the Spanish skies.

He was born in Cadiz on May 22, 1910. From a young age, he showed a great inclination for aviation, a passion that would lead him to enter the military aviation academy, where he trained as a fighter pilot. In those years, military aviation in Spain was still developing, but Salvador quickly stood out thanks to his skill and dedication, earning the trust of his superiors and the respect of his peers. When a coup d'état took place in 1936, which later led to the civil war, he joined the rebel side. In July 1936 he was named lieutenant of the XIX Tablada Breguet Group, the first in the IV Air Corps and his last promotion in aviation before the war. He quickly distinguished himself with the Nieuport 52 fighter plane loaned by the Parque Regional Sur and later with the Heinkel 51 imported from Germany, although his last performance would come piloting a Fiat CR32.

He was the top ace after García Morato, shooting down 23 planes and 1 balloon during the Civil War. He was shot down in the Ebro region in 1938 and imprisoned by the Republican Army in Catalonia until February 1939, when he was released after the end of the Catalan campaign. He flew 1,066 hours during the war, an average of 38 hours and 20 sorties per day.

Salvador y Díaz-Benjumea's success was not only due to his piloting skill but also to his ability to lead other pilots. He was known for being a leader committed to the instruction and training of his subordinates, which contributed to the development of an elite squadron among the nationalist ranks. His focus on tactical discipline and precision was key to reducing casualties and improving the effectiveness of his unit's air combat missions.

Throughout the war, Salvador rose through the military ranks through his merits and achievements, eventually assuming leadership positions in the Nationalist Air Force. In his role as commander, he not only led combat missions but also organized intensive training to improve the readiness of new pilots.

He was awarded the Personal Military Medal for his wartime exploits. After the Civil War, he was assigned to the Fiat Tablada group and soon assumed command of the Fighter School and joined the Luftwaffe in 1942. In 1969, he was appointed secretary of the Spanish Air Force where he served until 1974.

Second World War (1939–1945)

The Second World War marked a turning point in the history of aviation, transforming it into a crucial force on the battlefield and in the development of military strategies. During this conflict, aircraft not only supported troops on land and sea but also took the war to new horizons, in many cases deciding the course of the war on each front.

At the start of the conflict, the world's major powers had modernized air forces, and aviation quickly demonstrated its importance. The Battle of Britain (1940) was one of the first examples of a contest decided almost exclusively in the air, where the British Royal Air Force successfully defended its country from attacks by the German Luftwaffe. This victory not only allowed the Allies to maintain an essential base in Europe but also demonstrated that air superiority was essential in defense and attack.

Aviation enabled new tactics in ground warfare. Strategic bombers, such as the American B-17 Flying Fortress and the British Lancaster, carried out large-scale bombing campaigns against cities, factories, and supply lines, attempting to weaken the enemy's industrial and military power. At the same time, fighters and fighter-bombers, such as the P-51 Mustang and Spitfire, played vital roles in escorting these bombers and in air superiority. Aircraft were also key in the Pacific theaters, where aircraft carriers such as the USS Enterprise and Akagi allowed the projection of air power miles away. The Battle of Midway (1942) was decisive in this regard, where the United States

Navy, using carrier-based aircraft, managed to neutralize Japanese naval superiority.

For the first time in history, aviation was also used for psychological and terror warfare, as air attacks brought destruction directly to civilian populations, as in the bombings of London, Dresden, Hamburg, Hiroshima, and Nagasaki. This ability to strike from a distance consolidated the role of aviation in world military policy and developed the foundations for the Cold War.

In short, World War II demonstrated the power of aviation in combat, both as a tactical and strategic tool. Air superiority became a necessity for armed forces, and advances in air technology and tactics during this period continued to influence modern warfare.

One thing to note is the difference in the number of kills by the pilots on both sides. Although the Germans had more experience and more advanced aircraft at the beginning of the war, the truth is that their combat policies meant that they were in service for a long time and had very sporadic relief or rest breaks, unlike the Allied side, which flew fewer hours, and that meant that the Germans had more hours of battle, and therefore more opportunity to shoot down enemies.

1. Erich Hartmann: The greatest aviation ace in history

Erich Alfred Hartmann, known as "The Black Devil," by his enemies and "Bubi" by his colleagues, was born on April 19, 1922, in Weissach, Germany. He was the most successful fighter pilot of all time, with an astonishing record of 352 confirmed kills during World War II, an achievement that has not been surpassed.

Hartmann showed an interest in aviation from an early age, a talent he acquired from his mother, who was a pilot. In 1940, at the age of 18, he joined the Luftwaffe and began his flight training in 1941. His training coincided with the start of the Eastern Front, where the Luftwaffe was in desperate need of pilots to deal with the numerous Soviet aircraft.

In 1942, Hartmann was assigned to the 52nd Fighter Squadron (Jagdgeschwader 52), where he began his combat career. At first, he had a hard time adjusting and made mistakes that nearly cost him his life, but over time he developed an effective tactic that made him a legend. Hartmann was a master of patience, preferring to wait for the perfect moment to approach his opponent at close range before firing. This tactic minimized the risk of being detected and increased the likelihood of a successful shootdown.

During his years on the Eastern Front, Hartmann flew almost exclusively to the Messerschmitt Bf 109, a fighter he came to master to perfection. His skill and precision in combat allowed him to rack up an astonishing number of aerial victories, and he earned the respect of both his comrades and his enemies. In

1944, he was awarded the Knight's Cross of the Iron Cross with Oak Leaves, Swords and Diamonds, Germany's highest military decoration.

Despite his success in combat, Hartmann was known for his ethical approach and strict standards of conduct. He always avoided attacking pilots who abandoned their planes or aircraft in inferior flying conditions. He was also highly respected for his loyalty to his unit and his refusal to join the Nazi Party, which caused tensions with some senior officers.

In May 1945, following Germany's surrender, Hartmann was handed over to Soviet forces, where he suffered ten years of captivity in prisoner-of-war camps under harsh conditions. He was eventually released in 1955, after which he returned to West Germany and joined the newly formed German Air Force (Luftwaffe) of the Bundeswehr, serving as an instructor and high-ranking officer until his retirement in 1970.

Erich Hartmann passed away on September 20, 1993, in Weil im Schönbuch, Germany. His legacy as the most successful fighter ace remains a landmark in the history of military aviation. Hartmann is remembered for his unparalleled skill, courage, and unwavering commitment to his principles, becoming a legend in the world of aviation.

2. Gerhard Barkhorn: The Second Successful Ace in History

Gerhard "Gerd" Barkhorn, born March 20, 1919, in Königsberg, East Prussia, was one of the most prominent fighter pilots of the Luftwaffe during World War II. With 301 confirmed victories, Barkhorn is the second-highest flying ace of all time, surpassed only by his compatriot Erich Hartmann.

Barkhorn began his aviation career when he joined the Luftwaffe in 1937, where he was trained as a fighter pilot. When war broke out in 1939, Barkhorn took part in the invasion of France and the Battle of Britain, where he experienced his first combat experience. However, it was on the Eastern Front, during the invasion of the Soviet Union in 1941, that Barkhorn established himself as an exceptional pilot.

Unlike other aces, Barkhorn did not have an outstanding start to his career. It was months before he scored his first combat victory, and his progress was slow. However, over time, he developed a meticulous and patient approach to aerial combat that made him stand out. Barkhorn primarily flew the Messerschmitt Bf 109 and the Focke-Wulf Fw 190, two of the Luftwaffe's most powerful fighters, which he used for escort and attack missions against Soviet forces.

His skill and persistence led to an impressive number of victories, and in 1944 he was awarded the Knight's Cross of the Iron Cross with Oak Leaves and Swords, one of the highest German military distinctions. Despite his achievements, Barkhorn was not a rash pilot. He was known for his caution in combat, often preferring to avoid unnecessary risks and flying strategically to maximize his chances of success and survival.

Barkhorn served primarily in the 52nd Fighter Squadron (Jagdgeschwader 52), a unit renowned for producing some of the war's most accomplished aces. He was respected by his peers and superiors, who valued his skill and leadership in the air. During his career, Barkhorn flew more than 1,100 combat missions, an impressive number that reflects his dedication and endurance.

In January 1945, he was severely wounded in combat and spent time in hospital recovering from his wounds. At the end of the war, Barkhorn was captured by American forces, although he was released shortly after. After the war, Barkhorn continued his aviation career and joined the newly formed German Air Force (Luftwaffe) of the Bundeswehr, where he held several high-ranking positions.

Gerhard Barkhorn died on January 8, 1983, at the age of 63, in a car accident with his wife Christl. His legacy lives on as one of the most respected and successful fighter aces in the history of military aviation. Barkhorn is remembered not only for his numerical achievements, but also for his dedication, professionalism, and calm character, which made him an exemplary figure in German aviation in World War II.

3. Günther Rall: A Flying Ace and Luftwaffe Legend

Major Günther Rall was born on March 10, 1918, in Gaggenau, Germany. During his career as a fighter pilot in the Luftwaffe during World War II, Rall became the third most successful flying ace in history, with a total of 275 confirmed victories in aerial combat. His life is a tale of skill, courage, and recovery from numerous wounds sustained in combat.

Rall joined the Luftwaffe in 1936, inspired by his love of aviation and his desire to serve his country. After completing his flight training, he was assigned to No. 52 Fighter Squadron (Jagdgeschwader 52, or JG 52), a unit that would stand out as one of the most successful on the Eastern Front. His combat career began during the invasion of France in 1940 and continued in the Battle of Britain, where he learned from the challenges and lessons German pilots faced from the British Royal Air Force.

It was on the Eastern Front, however, during the German invasion of the Soviet Union, where Rall established himself as a formidable ace. Early in Operation Barbarossa in 1941, Rall experienced several victories and stood out as one of the best pilots in his unit. In November of that same year, following combat, his plane was shot down and Rall was severely wounded in the back, an injury that kept him hospitalized for several months. Against all odds, he recovered and, despite having to endure lifelong pain, returned to combat in 1942.

Rall's career took off again after his return to duty. By 1943, he had reached 100 victories, and later 200, earning him the Knight's Cross of the Iron Cross with Oak Leaves and Swords, one of Nazi Germany's highest honors. His skills in aerial combat and tenacity on the battlefield allowed him to adapt to Soviet tactics and maneuvers, which greatly contributed to his success in the air.

In late 1943, Rall was promoted and assigned to a new unit, where he continued to rack up victories and fight against the growing Allied air forces. In April 1944, while flying a mission over Romania, he was shot down again by American fighters and suffered a broken finger. This injury forced him into a period of recovery, although he returned to combat shortly after.

After the end of World War II, Rall was captured by the British and spent a brief period as a prisoner of war. He was subsequently released and began a new phase in his life. He eventually joined the newly formed German Air Force (Luftwaffe) in the Federal Republic of Germany and helped rebuild German military aviation in the post-war era. During the Cold War, Rall maintained good relations with the Allies and contributed to the formation and strengthening of NATO.

Günther Rall retired from the Air Force in 1975 and continued to participate in aviation-related events. Throughout his life, he was admired for his professionalism, exceptional skills, and perseverance. Rall passed away on October 4, 2009, at the age of 91, leaving a legacy of honor and courage in the history of military aviation. His career is notable not only for his achievements, but for his dedication and resilience, and he is remembered as one of the greatest pilots in the history of aviation.

4. Otto Kittel: History's Fourth Flying Ace

Otto Kittel was born on February 21, 1917, in Kronsdorf, Bohemia (then part of the Austro-Hungarian Empire). During World War II, he would become one of Luftwaffe's most successful pilots, scoring 267 confirmed victories in aerial combat, all of them on the Eastern Front. His skill and lethality in combat earned him a place among the most respected and feared aces of his time.

Kittel joined the Luftwaffe in 1939, when he was 22, and soon completed his training as a fighter pilot. In 1941, he was assigned to Fighter Squadron 54 (Jagdgeschwader 54), also known as the "Grünherz Squadron" or "Green Heart," and began flying on the Eastern Front, where the confrontation with the Soviet air forces was constant and lethal. It was in this theater that Kittel stood out as an exceptional pilot and became a key figure in the squadron.

Although the first years of his career were quiet, Kittel began to gain notoriety as he racked up combat victories. His first kill was recorded in the winter of 1941, and from then on, his skills in the air began to grow exponentially. Flying in a Messerschmitt Bf 109 fighter and then in the Focke-Wulf Fw 190, he demonstrated relentless precision and an incredible ability to maneuver, allowing him to rack up victories against Soviet pilots.

Unlike some aces, Kittel was reserved and preferred not to draw attention to his achievements, earning him the nickname "Silent Ace" among his peers. Although his low-key nature kept him out of the spotlight, his prowess was undisputed. In 1943, after reaching 100 victories, he was awarded the Knight's Cross of the Iron Cross. The following year, after surpassing 200 victories, he was awarded the Oak Leaves to his Knight's Cross, one of Germany's highest military honors.

Kittel continued to fly missions on the Eastern Front, facing increasingly better-trained and better-equipped Soviet aircraft and pilots. However, his ability to adapt to enemy tactics and his ability to survive increasing threats kept him as one of the most feared aces of the conflict. His last mission took place on February 14, 1945, in a confrontation over Soviet territory. During combat, his plane was hit, and Kittel was killed instantly, just a week shy of his 28th birthday.

Otto Kittel was the fourth most victorious fighter pilot in history, and his life and career reflect the harshness and constant danger of air combat on the Eastern Front. Although his name is not as well-known as that of other Luftwaffe aces, Kittel is still remembered as one of the most successful fighter pilots of World War II. His legacy is a testament to the skill, bravery, and resilience required to face one of the most intense stages of military aviation.

5. Walter Nowotny: The Luftwaffe Ace with 258 Victories

Walter "Nowi" Nowotny was one of the most decorated Luftwaffe flying aces during World War II, racking up a total of 258 victories in air combat. Born on December 7, 1920, in Gmünd, Austria, Nowotny was known for his outstanding skills and bravery on the battlefield. His name is remembered in aviation history for his brilliant career and his impact on air tactics.

Nowotny joined the Luftwaffe in 1939, at age 19, shortly after Austria was annexed by Germany. He was assigned to Fighter Squadron 54 (Jagdgeschwader 54, or JG 54), also known as the "Grünherz" (Green Heart). His combat career began in 1941 when the Luftwaffe was deployed to the Eastern Front during the German invasion of the Soviet Union in Operation Barbarossa. However, his first months at the front were not easy: on his first mission, his plane was hit by enemy fire, and he had to make an emergency landing in the Gulf of Riga, surviving three days on a raft in icy waters before being rescued. This experience marked the beginning of a career full of successes and challenges.

From 1942, Nowotny began to rack up victories rapidly, reaching 50 and then 100 combat victories in a surprisingly short time. His precision and fearlessness earned him the Knight's Cross in 1943 when he had already surpassed 150 victories. In the summer of that year, his skills led him to become the first pilot in history to reach the impressive figure of 250 victories, an achievement that earned him recognition from the Luftwaffe and the Oak Leaves,

Swords and Diamonds to his Knight's Cross, one of Nazi Germany's highest distinctions.

Nowotny was known for his prowess in aerial combat and his ability to adapt to enemy tactics, making him a lethal pilot. His preferred fighter was the Focke-Wulf Fw 190, which he handled with great skill in high-speed combat and aerobatic maneuvers. In September 1943, he was transferred to a training role due to his impressive achievements, but in 1944 he was called back into action and assigned to the testing unit for new jet technology in the Jet Fighter Squadron (Erprobungskommando 262).

This squadron used the revolutionary Messerschmitt Me 262, the world's first operational jet fighter. Nowotny was one of the first to fly this aircraft in combat, and despite the technical challenges, he achieved several additional victories with this new model. However, on November 8, 1944, on a mission with the Me 262, his aircraft was attacked by a group of American fighters and shot down near Hesepe, Germany. Nowotny died in the incident, aged 23.

Walter Nowotny's life left a remarkable legacy in the history of military aviation. He was an exceptional pilot and one of the first to explore the potential of jets in aerial combat, representing a milestone in the evolution of military aviation. Although he died young, his bravery, skills, and achievements established him as one of the most decorated and legendary aces of the Luftwaffe during World War II.

6. Heinz Bär: German World War II Flying Ace

Heinz "Pritzl" Bär was one of the most notable pilots of the German Luftwaffe during World War II, with an impressive record of 221 confirmed aerial victories in over 1,000 combat missions. Known for his great piloting skill and extraordinary marksmanship, Bär was a key figure in the air war over Europe and North Africa, excelling in both defensive and offensive combat.

Heinz Bär was born on March 25, 1913, in Sommerfeld, Germany (now Lubusz, Poland). Although his beginnings were humble, he developed a strong interest in aviation from a young age. He began his career in the military in 1934, enlisting in the aviation service, and was then selected to train as a pilot in the Luftwaffe, the newly formed air force of the Third Reich.

Bär was initially assigned to JG 51, a Luftwaffe fighter unit, and took part in the invasion of France and the Battle of Britain. During the latter, he demonstrated great skill and bravery, managing to shoot down several British aircraft and quickly gained a reputation as a formidable pilot.

With the outbreak of the campaigns in North Africa and the Eastern Front, Bär was transferred to fighter units stationed in these combat theaters. Flying primarily the Messerschmitt Bf 109 and later the Focke-Wulf Fw 190, Bär scored 96 of his victories on the Eastern Front and also demonstrated his skills in the air war over the Mediterranean. His attack technique and ability to adapt to different environments made him a versatile and highly effective pilot.

Heinz Bär was known for his great precision and coolness in combat. He always preferred to conserve his ammunition and attack his enemies from optimal distances. His ability to handle his aircraft in difficult situations and close combat made him almost invincible in the air. As he gained experience, he improved his combat techniques and developed the tactics that he shared with his comrades.

Throughout his career, Bär was transferred to several fighter units, including JG 3 and JG 1. Late in the war, he joined a jet fighter test unit and became one of the few German pilots to fly the Messerschmitt Me 262, the world's first jet fighter aircraft. In Me 262, he achieved 16 additional victories, becoming one of the leading aces in this innovative aircraft.

Throughout his career, Bär received multiple decorations, most notably the Knight's Cross of the Iron Cross with Oak Leaves and Swords, one of the highest military distinctions in Nazi Germany, awarded only to the most successful and experienced pilots. He was recognized numerous times for his leadership and bravery, and his combat skills were an inspiration to other German pilots.

At the end of the war, Heinz Bär was captured by Allied forces and spent some time in captivity before being released. After the war, Bär kept a low profile and avoided involvement in political or military matters. He was tragically killed in a plane crash on 28 April 1957 while conducting a test flight in a light aircraft.

Heinz Bär is remembered as one of the Luftwaffe's most talented fighter pilots and one of the most successful flying aces in history. His legacy remains an example of skill, endurance, and tactical ability in aerial combat. Through his achievements and victories, Bär left a mark on aviation history, and his life and career continue to be studied by historians and military aviation enthusiasts.

7. Richard Bong: America's Greatest Flying Ace of World War II

Richard Ira Bong, known as America's "Ace of Aces," was born on September 24, 1920, in Superior, Wisconsin. During World War II, he stood out as one of the United States Army Air Force's deadliest pilots, scoring 40 victories in aerial combat, making him the American pilot with the most confirmed kills in history.

From a young age, Bong showed an interest in aviation and an innate ability to fly. In 1941, he joined the U.S. Army Air Force and received training on the advanced Lockheed P-38 Lightning fighter plane, a twin-engine fighter known for its speed and maneuverability. His first assignment was in the Pacific Theater, where the fierce air war against Japan was escalating.

Bong began flying missions in 1942, and very soon proved his skills in combat. He was known for his bravery and deadly accuracy in attacking enemy aircraft. Over the next two years, he racked up victories, surpassing the 20-shootdown mark in 1943, making him one of the most successful aces of the conflict. In recognition of his achievements, he was awarded the Distinguished Flying Cross and the Silver Star.

As his fame grew, so did his number of victories. By early 1944, he had reached 30 victories, and in August of that year, he shot down his 40th enemy aircraft, securing his place as America's top flying ace. This achievement earned him the Medal of Honor, the United States' highest military decoration, awarded personally by General Douglas MacArthur. However, due to the high risk involved in keeping him in combat, Bong was withdrawn from the front in November 1944 and returned to the United States, where he became a national hero and participated in war bond promotion campaigns.

Although Bong might have retired from active duty, his passion for aviation did not wane. In 1945, he was assigned as a test pilot in California, working the innovative Lockheed P-80 Shooting Star jet, America's first jet fighter. Unfortunately, on August 6, 1945, during a test flight of the P-80, Bong's plane experienced a mechanical failure and crashed, resulting in his tragic death at the age of 24.

Richard Bong left behind a legacy of bravery, skill, and dedication to service. His extraordinary record of 40 victories made him a symbol of heroism and prowess for American military aviation. To this day, he is remembered as America's ace of aces and one of the most accomplished fighter pilots of World War II.

8. Ivan Kozhedub: The Greatest Soviet Flying Ace

Born on June 8, 1920, in the small Ukrainian town of Obrazhiyivka, Ivan Nikitovich Kozhedub was the Soviet Union's most successful fighter pilot during World War II. With a record of 62 confirmed aerial victories, he is widely regarded as one of the greatest fighter pilots of all time. His extraordinary combat ability and skill in handling the Lavochkin La-5 fighter and later the La-7 earned him the title of Soviet Ace of Aces and the decoration of Hero of the Soviet Union three times, one of the highest honors in the country.

Kozhedub began his military career in 1940 when he joined the Chuguev aviation school in Ukraine. After completing his training, he was assigned as a flight instructor, a role that kept him out of combat. However, in early 1943, with the war at its height, Kozhedub was transferred to the front and began flying combat missions on the Eastern Front as part of the 240th Fighter Aviation Regiment.

In July 1943, during the famous Battle of Kursk, Kozhedub achieved his first aerial victory. From that point on, his skill became evident, and he began to stand out as one of the best pilots in the Soviet Air Force. In each engagement with the Luftwaffe, he demonstrated his bravery and precision, scoring kills of both Messerschmitt Bf 109 fighters and the famous Focke-Wulf Fw 190.

Kozhedub was known for his exceptional marksmanship and maneuverability, qualities that helped him excel in intense aerial combat. In 1944, his victories increased rapidly, and in March 1945 he reached a personal record with 62 confirmed kills, all of them German fighter aircraft. His exceptional combat performance earned him the Order of the Red Banner and the title of Hero of the Soviet Union on three occasions (1944, 1944, and 1945), an honor reserved only for the most distinguished Soviet soldiers.

In addition to his victories against the Luftwaffe, Kozhedub also encountered American aircraft in special circumstances. On a mission towards the end of the war, he was confronted by two American P-51 Mustang fighters which mistakenly opened fire on him. Kozhedub had no choice but to defend himself, and both American fighters were shot down in an incident that remained secret for many years to avoid diplomatic tensions.

After the end of World War II, Kozhedub continued to serve in the Soviet Air Force. During the Korean War, although he did not directly participate in combat, he played an important role as commander of a Soviet fighter unit assisting North Korean forces. At the end of his military career, he was promoted to the rank of Air Marshal, a highly prestigious title in the Soviet Union.

Ivan Kozhedub passed away on 8 August 1991, just before the dissolution of the Soviet Union, but his legacy lives on. To this day, Kozhedub is remembered as the Soviet Union's most successful fighter pilot and one of the greatest aces in aviation history, with a record of bravery and skill that has made him a symbol of Soviet resistance during World War II.

9. Saburo Sakai: The Imperial Japanese Flying Ace

Saburo Sakai was one of the most well-known and respected Japanese flying aces during World War II, racking up at least 64 confirmed victories. He was born on August 25, 1916, in Saga, Japan, to a farming family. Wanting to escape poverty and achieve a better future, Sakai joined the Imperial Japanese Navy in 1933, and, after excelling in his training, entered the pilot program in 1937.

Sakai graduated at the top of his class, and by 1938 he was flying the Mitsubishi A5M, the precursor to the famous A6M Zero, in the Second Sino-Japanese War. By 1941, Sakai had gained experience and was soon assigned to Tainan Air Base in Formosa (present-day Taiwan), from where he began operating in the Pacific Theater during World War II. Piloting the legendary Mitsubishi A6M Zero, Sakai soon became renowned for his precision and prowess in aerial combat. In the early months of the war, during campaigns in the Philippines and the Dutch East Indies, Sakai racked up dozens of victories, earning the admiration of his peers and superiors.

On August 7, 1942, at the Battle of Guadalcanal, Sakai had one of his most trying experiences. Facing a formation of American bombers and their escorting fighters, he was severely wounded in the head and arm by enemy fire, leaving him blind in his right eye. Despite his injuries, Sakai managed to maneuver his Zero and fly for more than four hours to return to his base in Rabaul, New Britain. This feat of endurance and skill made him a legend.

After a long recovery, Sakai returned to flying in combat in 1944, and despite his visual impairment, he continued to fly missions with notable success. However, wartime conditions had changed, and Japan faced larger and better-equipped air forces, making it difficult for Japanese aviation to achieve victories.

Throughout the war, Sakai showed special respect for enemy pilots. He was known for his decision not to fire on American pilots who abandoned combat or showed signs of surrender, a move that was unusual among pilots of the time and reflected the samurai code of honor with which he was raised.

After Japan's surrender in 1945, Sakai worked as a printer and became a man of peace. For the rest of his life, he devoted much of his time to honoring his fallen comrades and promoting understanding between former enemies. He also wrote his autobiography, Samurai, which recounted his experience as a pilot in World War II and his transformation.

Saburo Sakai died on September 22, 2000, at the age of 84. His life and accomplishments made him one of Japan's most iconic flying aces, remembered for both his bravery in combat and his humanity.

10. Kurt Welter: The Luftwaffe's Night Ace

Kurt Welter, born February 25, 1916, in Cologne, Germany, was a prominent Luftwaffe fighter pilot during World War II, known primarily for his specialization in night combat. Welter is remembered as one of the most successful night flying aces, racking up around 63 confirmed victories, of which approximately 56 were achieved during night missions, making him the night ace with the most victories in history.

Welter began his career in the Luftwaffe as a mechanic in 1934 and later trained as a pilot, standing out for his skills and precision. In 1943, he joined the night fighter units, just as the British Royal Air Force's night bombing raids on Germany were at their height. He soon joined the Nachtjagdgeschwader (NJG) squadron, which specialized in intercepting enemy bombers on night flights, a task that required not only great flying skill but also the ability to operate in dark conditions and disorienting environments, as well as an excellent sense of direction.

In 1944, Welter began flying the revolutionary Messerschmitt Me 262 jet fighter, the world's first jet fighter to see combat and became one of the few pilots to employ it effectively on night missions. The Me 262 was fast, maneuverable, and equipped for high-altitude, high-speed missions, making it especially effective against Allied bombers. However, flying the Me 262 at night required exceptional skill due to the aircraft's speed and the complications of flying in poor visibility.

Welter quickly excelled in using the Me 262 and established a special night fighter unit called Kommando Welter, which specialized in intercepting British night bombers, primarily Lancasters and Mosquitos. Even though the Me 262 was not equipped with radar suitable for night flight, Welter relied on his experience and ability to detect and shoot down enemy bombers in complete darkness.

Welter's precision in these engagements earned him recognition among his peers and superiors, and he was awarded the Knight's Cross of the Iron Cross in 1945, one of the Luftwaffe's highest honors.

By the end of the war, Kurt Welter was regarded as one of the Luftwaffe's most successful aces in night missions and the night pilot with the most victories in a jet fighter, amassing a total of 63 confirmed victories throughout his career. Despite his great success as a pilot, the war left deep scars, and after the end of the conflict, Welter retired from military life.

Kurt Welter died in 1949, shortly after the war, in little-known circumstances. Today, he is remembered as one of the pioneers in night aviation and the use of jet fighters in combat, leaving a legacy in the history of military aviation and marking a milestone in the evolution of night combat air tactics.

11. Lev Lvovich Shestakov: Soviet World War II Flying Ace

Lev Lvovich Shestakov was one of the leading Soviet aviation aces during World War II, scoring a remarkable 39 confirmed kills. His bravery, skills, and determination in combat earned him a prominent place in Soviet aviation history and on the list of World War II aces. Throughout his career, Shestakov demonstrated exceptional aerial combat ability and earned the respect of his peers and superiors.

Lev Shestakov was born on December 22, 1915, in the village of Karlovka in present-day Ukraine, then part of the Russian Empire. From a young age, he showed an interest in aviation, influenced by the growing importance of the Soviet Air Force in the 1930s. He entered a military flight school, where he excelled in his piloting skills and technical knowledge.

After graduating, Shestakov was assigned to a Soviet Air Force fighter unit. His skills were quickly noticed by his superiors, who groomed him to become an elite fighter pilot and leader. He was assigned to the front lines at the start of the German invasion of the Soviet Union in 1941 and joined the fight to defend his homeland from the advancing Third Reich.

With the start of Operation Barbarossa, the German invasion of the Soviet Union in June 1941, Shestakov was called upon to confront the Nazi threat on the Eastern Front. He quickly became one of the most effective pilots in the Soviet Air Force, racking up kills and victorious engagements. His prowess as a fighter pilot brought him into combat with the Luftwaffe's Messerschmitt Bf 109 and Focke-Wulf Fw 190, aircraft that posed a considerable threat to Soviet forces.

Shestakov flew aircraft such as the Yakovlev Yak-1, an agile and maneuverable fighter that suited his style of combat well. His ability to maneuver and skill in close combat allowed him to outmaneuver numerous enemy pilots. In a series of decisive air battles, Shestakov demonstrated an aggressive approach and outstanding skill, which helped him rack up an impressive kill tally.

In addition to his skills as a pilot, Shestakov excelled as a leader and strategist in the air. As his combat experience increased, he assumed leadership positions in his squadron, sharing tactics and training younger pilots. His focus on precision and tactical discipline was key to his success and the success of his fellow pilots in combat.

Shestakov applied a combination of group combat tactics and aggressive close combat maneuvers to engage German fighter formations. These tactics helped his unit achieve a high success rate on missions, even in the most adverse conditions. Through his leadership, Shestakov inspired other pilots to face the Luftwaffe with renewed confidence and determination.

Lev Shestakov achieved a total of 39 confirmed aerial victories during World War II, an achievement that made him one of the leading Soviet aces. He was decorated with multiple awards, including the Order of Lenin and the Order of the Red Star, honors given for his bravery and dedication to the service of the Soviet Union. His contribution was crucial to the defense of the country and the numerous victories of the Soviet Air Force throughout the conflict.

Sadly, Shestakov was killed in action in 1944, during a mission on the Eastern Front. Although his life was cut short prematurely, his legacy and contributions to the Soviet war effort remained etched in the memories of his countrymen and the records of military aviation.

12. Gregory "Pappy" Boyington. The Ace of the Pacific

Gregory "Pappy" Boyington was one of the most iconic pilots of World War II, known as much for his combat skill as for his eccentric character and strong personality. As the leader of the famed "Black Sheep" fighter squadron (VMF-214) of the United States Marines, Boyington distinguished himself in the Pacific theater, racking up 28 confirmed victories against Japanese aircraft and earning a reputation for bravery and tenacity in combat.

Gregory Boyington was born on December 4, 1912, in Coeur d'Alene, Idaho, and raised in Tacoma, Washington. From a young age, he showed an interest in sports and aviation and was known for his rebellious spirit. He attended the University of Washington, where he was part of the wrestling team, and graduated with a degree in aeronautical engineering in 1934.

As a child, Greg's parents divorced and he grew up with his stepfather's last name, Hallenbeck. However, when he decided to enroll in flight school, he asked for his birth certificate and discovered that his father was Charles Boyington, a dentist, from whom he would take his last name.

After completing his studies, Boyington joined the United States Marine Corps and was trained as a pilot. In his early years, he demonstrated exceptional skills in handling fighter aircraft but also showed a penchant for breaking rules and a strong temper that brought him into conflict with some superiors.

At the start of World War II, Boyington decided to temporarily leave the Marine Corps to join the "Flying Tigers", an American mercenary unit organized by Claire Lee Chennault to support China against the Japanese invasion. With the Flying Tigers, Boyington had the opportunity to fly the Curtiss P-40 and achieved six confirmed victories, which reinforced his combat ability and his experience against Japanese aircraft.

However, his time with the Flying Tigers was not without problems; his conflicts with discipline and his drinking problems complicated his relationships with other pilots and with Chennault. In 1942, Boyington left the group and returned to the Marine Corps.

Back in the Marine Corps, Boyington was assigned to VMF-214, known as the "Black Sheep." This squadron was made up primarily of young and sometimes undisciplined pilots, allowing Boyington to adapt his informal and bold leadership style. As commander, Boyington inspired his men to fight with determination, and his experience with the Flying Tigers allowed him to devise effective strategies to confront the Japanese pilots.

Under his command, VMF-214 achieved great success in the Pacific campaign. Boyington particularly excelled in the Battle of the Solomon Islands, scoring multiple kills of Japanese aircraft. His aggressiveness in combat, his ability to anticipate enemy movements, and his knowledge of Japanese aircraft tactics made him one of the most feared pilots in the region. In total, he racked up 28 aerial victories, becoming one of the leading American aviation aces.

On January 3, 1944, during a mission over Rabaul, Boyington was shot down by Japanese fighters and captured. He spent nearly 20 months as a prisoner of war in various Japanese prisons, where he endured extremely harsh conditions, food shortages, and abuse. His health deteriorated markedly, but he managed to survive until he was released at the end of the war in 1945.

Upon his return to the United States, Boyington was welcomed as a hero. In 1945, he was awarded the Medal of Honor for his heroic actions and outstanding skill as a pilot. He also received the Navy Cross and other awards for his wartime service.

Boyington's life after the war was complicated, however. The transition to civilian life was difficult, and he had problems with alcohol that affected his health and personal relationships. Nonetheless, he wrote an autobiography titled Baa Baa Black Sheep, in which he recounted his wartime experiences, which would later inspire a popular television series.

Gregory "Pappy" Boyington is remembered as one of the most colorful and talented aces of World War II. His combat skills, bold leadership, and unwavering personality made him a legend among American fighter pilots. Despite his flaws, Boyington left a legacy of bravery and determination that remains an inspiration to military and civilian aviators.

Aviation in the Korean War (1950-1953)

The Korean War (1950-1953) was a significant conflict in the history of military aviation, marking the first major confrontation of the Cold War and a turning point in air technology and tactics. The war represented the combat debut of jet aircraft from both sides, redefining the nature of air combat and providing a critical test for the technological advances achieved after World War II.

From the beginning of the conflict, aviation was a crucial factor in the intervention of the U.S.-led UN forces. With the dominance of the air, US air forces, especially the newly created Strategic Air Command and the United States Air Force (USAF), played a leading role in reconnaissance operations, attacks on enemy targets, and support for South Korean and UN ground forces. Fighter aircraft such as the F-80 Shooting Star and B-29 Superfortress carried out strategic bombing operations to weaken the logistical and military capabilities of North Korean and Chinese communist forces.

The war brought one of the earliest and most significant deployments of jet aircraft in combat. The F-86 Sabre, a state-of-the-art jet fighter for the time, proved to be a formidable fighter in high-altitude combat, establishing a victory record that outstripped its adversaries in the Korean theater. American forces leveraged the Sabre to tactical advantage, especially in the "MiG Alley" area, a strip of airspace over the Yalu River where some of the most intense air combat of the war took place.

China's intervention and Soviet support for North Korea included the dispatch of MiG-15 aircraft and the involvement of unofficial Soviet pilots, who flew under Chinese or North Korean identifications to avoid direct conflict with the United States. Introduced into combat in the late 1950s, the MiG-15s changed the dynamics of aerial engagement, being faster and able to operate at higher altitudes than earlier American fighters. These jet fighters soon became a significant threat to UN aircraft and forced the United States to introduce F-86 Sabre fighters, which were a match for the MiG-15 in terms of speed, maneuverability, and firepower.

The clashes between the F-86 and the MiG-15 were intense, and these fighters' marked history as the protagonists of the first major combat between jet aircraft. Pilots from both sides, such as the American Joseph McConnell and the Soviet Nikolay Sutyagin, became air aces by obtaining numerous victories in the skies of Korea, demonstrating their skills in this new type of combat.

The Korean War was key to the development and refinement of tactics and technologies that would later be standard in Cold War conflicts. At the tactical level, the fighting in MiG Alley underlined the importance of ground-based radar coordination, real-time communication, and the need to develop advanced countermeasures against enemy missiles and radars. The pilots' experience in these engagements also highlighted the importance of maneuverability and reaction speed in combat, influencing the design of future generations of jet fighters.

Air dominance also became a propaganda resource, as both the United States and the Soviet Union sought to highlight the skills of their pilots and jet fighters. Coverage of the exploits of the air aces in the media of both blocs had a motivational effect on their respective populations and served as a symbol of the technological and military superiority that each side aspired to demonstrate during the Cold War.

The Korean War was a decisive conflict for modern military aviation, standing out as the stage where jet fighters were consolidated, and air combat tactics were redefined. Although the conflict left the Korean peninsula divided and with much of its infrastructure devastated, its effects on military aviation and technology continued to impact Cold War developments and set the path for combat aviation in the decades that followed. The experience gained and lessons learned in Korea helped shape an era of innovation in military aviation that continues to this day.

1. Nikolai Sutyagin: The Ace of the Korean War

Nikolai Vasilievich Sutyagin, born on May 5, 1923, in Smagino, a small town in eastern Russia, is remembered as one of the Soviet Union's most prominent aviation aces, particularly for his role in the Korean War. Sutyagin rose to fame by becoming the fighter pilot with the most confirmed kills during that conflict, achieving a total of 21 aerial victories in combat between jet fighters, making him one of the most successful aces of jet age.

Sutyagin joined the Soviet Air Force in 1941, and after years of training and dedication, he became a fighter pilot. During his early career, he flew various models of Soviet fighter aircraft, and with the outbreak of the Korean War in 1950, he was assigned to the Korean Front as part of a secret mission of Soviet pilots operating under Korean or Chinese identities. The Soviet Union avoided direct official involvement in the conflict to avoid open confrontation with the United States; however, they did send MiG-15 aircraft and their best pilots, including Sutyagin, to support North Korea and China.

Sutyagin flew the famous MiG-15 jet fighter, an aircraft that was at the forefront of fighter technology at the time. This aircraft regularly clashed with the US Air Force's F-86 Sabre, and the MiG-15 vs. F-86 fights became the first major duel of jet age. With the MiG-15, Sutyagin demonstrated exceptional combat prowess, standing out for his ability to maneuver at high speed and his precision in attacks. His intimate knowledge of the MiG-15 allowed him to successfully engage Sabre pilots, many of whom were also highly experienced veterans.

Throughout the war, Sutyagin racked up victories against American bombers and fighters. His record of 21 kills confirmed his place at the top of the Korean War's air aces. Sutyagin's combat prowess earned him the respect of both his peers and rivals and he was regarded as a calculating and strategic pilot, able to anticipate enemy movements and take advantage of every opportunity in combat.

After the Korean War, Sutyagin continued his career in the Soviet Air Force and became a legend within Soviet military aviation circles. However, due to the secretive nature of the Soviet intervention in Korea, his exploits were not made public until many years after the conflict, as the Soviet Union kept its involvement in the war under strict secrecy during the Cold War.

Nikolai Sutyagin passed away on November 12, 1986, but his legacy lives on as one of the most successful aviation aces in jet history. His participation in the Korean War and his record of victories position him as a symbol of the skill and dedication of Soviet fighter pilots during one of the tensest times of the 20th century.

2. Yevgeny Pepelyaev: Korean War Ace

Yevgeny Georgievich Pepelyaev, born March 18, 1918, in Bodaybo, Siberia, was one of the Soviet Union's most prominent aces during the Korean War, racking up 19 confirmed victories in aerial combat. His skill and ability in handling MiG-15 made him one of the most successful pilots of that era, and his achievements in the conflict positioned him as one of the great aces of Soviet aviation.

Pepelyaev joined the Soviet Air Force in 1938 and, after his training, participated in World War II, although he did not rack up any aerial victories in that conflict due to his role as an instructor in the eastern Soviet Union. After the war, Pepelyaev continued his aviation career, and, by 1950, he had become an experienced jet fighter pilot. He was appointed commander of the 196th Fighter Aviation Regiment in the Korean War, a unit equipped with the new and advanced MiG-15 fighter.

In the context of the Korean War, the Soviet Union chose to covertly engage in support of North Korea and China, sending Soviet pilots such as Pepelyaev, who operated in the famous "MiG Alley," an area above the Yalu River where intense dogfights took place between Soviet MiG-15s and US Air Force F-86 Sabres. Pepelyaev, flying the MiG-15, proved to be an outstanding pilot in engagements against American fighters, at a time when jet-to-jet duels were still new terrain in air combat.

Pepelyaev racked up his 19 victories against a variety of UN aircraft types, including the F-86 Sabre, P-51 Mustang, and F-84 Thunderjet, all flown by experienced U.S. and allied airmen. His success was due to his accurate firing and skillful maneuvering, taking full advantage of MiG-15's high-speed and agility characteristics. Pepelyaev was known not only for his skills as a pilot but also as an exemplary leader who inspired confidence in his subordinates, leading his regiment effectively and courageously in one of the most intense conflicts of the Cold War.

Throughout the Korean War, Pepelyaev maintained his record of victories, establishing himself as one of the most respected aces.

After his return to the Soviet Union, Pepelyaev received numerous decorations for his service, including the prestigious Order of the Red Banner. After the war, he continued his career in military aviation and was promoted to various positions until his retirement. After retiring from military life, Pepelyaev lived quietly, keeping a low profile and enjoying his family life.

Yevgeny Pepelyaev passed away on January 4, 2013, at the age of 94, one of the last great Soviet aviation aces of his generation. His legacy in military aviation remains a testament to the skill and bravery of Soviet pilots in a conflict that marked a pivotal moment in the history of air combat and the Cold War.

3. James Jabara: America's First Jet Ace

James "Jabby" Jabara, born October 10, 1923, in Muskogee, Oklahoma, was a pioneering American pilot, recognized as the first jet fighter ace in the history of the United States Air Force and one of the most celebrated pilots of the Korean War. The son of Lebanese immigrants, Jabara grew up with a fascination for airplanes and a strong determination to fly for his country. He joined the United States Army Air Force in 1942, amid World War II, and was assigned to the role of fighter pilot.

During World War II, Jabara flew P-51 Mustang fighter planes and logged numerous hours of flight time, although he did not achieve any combat victories during that time. However, he distinguished himself by his skill and ability in escort and ground attack missions, skills that would make him a leading pilot in the following decade.

When the Korean War broke out in 1950, Jabara, already an experienced pilot, was assigned to the conflict as part of the United States Air Force's 4th Fighter Group. Equipped with the new F-86 Sabre jet fighter, Jabara joined dogfights against communist North Koreans, Chinese, and Soviets. It was in this context that Jabara excelled, demonstrating exceptional skill in taking on the MiG-15s, which at the time were some of the Soviet Union's most advanced fighter aircraft.

On May 20, 1951, Jabara achieved the distinction of being the first jet ace in American military history by scoring five confirmed victories over MiG-15 fighters. Throughout the Korean War, Jabara racked up a total of 15 kills, all of them of MiG-15 aircraft, establishing himself as one of the Air Force's most successful and recognized aces. His precision in combat and ability to maneuver the F-86 Sabre in fast and dangerous engagements earned him a reputation for bravery and combat prowess.

His success in Korea was not only a personal achievement, but also boosted the morale of the United States Air Force and underlined the effectiveness of the F-86 Sabre in battle against Soviet fighters. Jabara was awarded the Distinguished Service Cross and the Silver Star, among other military honors, and became an iconic figure for American Cold War pilots.

After his return from Korea, Jabara continued his career in the Air Force, rising to the rank of lieutenant colonel. However, his life was tragically cut short when, on November 17, 1966, he was killed in a car accident in Delray Beach, Florida, while traveling with his daughter Carol Ann, who also lost her life.

James Jabara left a legacy in American military aviation. His achievement as the first jet ace symbolizes a pivotal moment in military aviation history, marking the transition from the propeller age to the jet age and cementing America's role in dominating high-speed aerial combat.

The Role of Aviation in the Vietnam War (1955-1975)

The Vietnam War (1955-1975) marked one of the most complex and strategically demanding periods for military aviation. This conflict, in which the United States was heavily involved in support of the South Vietnamese government against North Vietnam and the Viet Cong guerrillas, required the extensive and diverse use of aviation, which was fundamental in the fields of combat, reconnaissance, transport, and in the implementation of massive bombing tactics. However, the nature and geography of the conflict in Vietnam also revealed the limitations of modern aviation in guerrilla warfare and jungle terrain.

One of the key elements of the US strategy was Operation Rolling Thunder, a massive aerial bombardment of North Vietnam between 1965 and 1968. This campaign aimed to destroy infrastructure and supply lines and to weaken the morale of the North Vietnamese. Using bombers such as the B-52

Stratofortress and F-105 Thunderchief, air strikes inflicted great destruction on strategic areas, although the results were limited due to North Vietnam's resilience and ability to build anti-aircraft defense systems, with the help of the Soviet Union.

North Vietnam developed a sophisticated air defense system that included radars, surface-to-air missiles (SAMs), and MiG-17 and MiG-21 fighters. American pilots faced a dangerous combination of anti-aircraft fire and enemy aircraft, making North Vietnam's airspace highly hostile territory. The creation of the U.S. Navy's Fighter Weapons School, known as Top Gun, arose as a response to deficiencies in air combat tactics and was instrumental in improving pilot performance in the war.

In the jungle and difficult mountainous terrain of Vietnam, close air support tactics proved essential to U.S. and Allied ground forces. Attack aircraft such as the A-1 Skyraider and F-4 Phantom II played a crucial role in these types of operations, supporting troops on the front lines by attacking enemy positions. Also critical was the use of helicopters, which transformed combat logistics. UH-1 "Huey" aircraft became an icon of the war, transporting troops, evacuating the wounded, and providing fire support in quick raids.

Aviation also facilitated rapid mobility and the extraction of soldiers in isolated locations or while fighting. These "air cavalry" operations allowed U.S. forces to launch attacks on strategic locations quickly, although, over time, Vietnamese guerrillas learned to hide and build tunnels to protect themselves from aerial bombardment.

Reconnaissance aircraft, using aircraft such as the U-2 and SR-71 Blackbird, provided U.S. commanders with crucial information about enemy positions movements, and activities on the Ho Chi Minh Trail, a complex supply system that connected North Vietnam to its forces in the south. Reconnaissance missions were dangerous, as reconnaissance aircraft often flew over hostile territory and were exposed to anti-aircraft fire.

In addition, electronic warfare operations were heavily employed, with specialized aircraft such as the EB-66 Destroyer jamming enemy radars and hampering the response capabilities of North Vietnamese air defenses.

During the conflict, U.S. forces used unconventional weapons such as napalm and Agent Orange. These agents were used to clear vegetation and expose enemy routes in the jungle, as well as to attempt to cut off the food supply of Viet Cong fighters. However, the use of napalm and Agent Orange caused devastating damage to the environment and had tragic effects on the Vietnamese civilian population, generating a controversy that persists to this day.

The Vietnam War demonstrates both the power and limitations of military aviation in guerrilla-type conflicts. Despite air and technological superiority, the United States was unable to defeat the enemy due to factors beyond aviation, such as guerrilla resistance and hostile terrain. Mass bombing tactics and close air support were effective at times, but the conflict demonstrated that victory in this type of warfare required not only air power but also a deep understanding of strategy and local context.

Aviation in Vietnam marked a turning point in the way conflicts would be managed in the future, and tactics, training, and technology evolved significantly in the aftermath of this experience. The Vietnam War left profound lessons for military aviation, and many of the tactics developed in that conflict influence air doctrine to this day.

1. Nguyen Van Coc: North Vietnamese Flying Ace

Born on February 14, 1942, in Dong Anh District outside Hanoi, North Vietnam, Nguyen Van Coc became the greatest flying ace of the Vietnam conflict and one of the most successful pilots in modern history. With a total of 9 to 11 confirmed victories over American aircraft, his prowess in aerial combat helped consolidate North Vietnam's aerial resistance to the powerful US Air Force and Navy.

Nguyen Van Coc grew up in a country scarred by occupation and war, first with the French and then with the Americans. As a young man, he observed the effects of the conflict up close and decided to join the Vietnam People's Air Force, training as a fighter pilot. He was sent to the Soviet Union to hone his skills and become familiar with the Soviet-made MiG-17 and MiG-21 fighters that would become the backbone of North Vietnam's air defense.

Returning to North Vietnam, Cốc joined the 921st Fighter Aviation Regiment, which was responsible for defending North Vietnamese airspace, especially the highly contested "MiG Alley" over the Red River north of Hanoi. The North Vietnamese Air Force's combat tactics were based on quick engagements and taking advantage of the MiG-21's speed and maneuverability to intercept American fighters and bombers.

Between 1967 and 1968, during the height of the Vietnam War, Cốc flew several successful sorties. His prowess with the MiG-21 and his precision in using K-13 air-to-air missiles allowed him to shoot down several American aircraft, including F-4 Phantoms and F-105 Thunderchiefs, quickly earning him a reputation as one of the most dangerous pilots in the region. Aerial ambush tactics, familiarity with the terrain, and a hit-and-run strategy were key to his success.

During his combat career, he is credited with between 9 and 11 confirmed victories, making him the most successful North Vietnamese. Most of his victories were against high-profile aircraft, flown by some of the best American aviators of the time. His skills earned him important decorations, including the People's Armed Forces Hero Medal and other awards for bravery and effectiveness on the battlefield.

Nguyen Van Coc retired from military aviation at the end of the war, leaving a legacy of resilience and skill that lives on in Vietnam's military history. His success in combat represents not only a personal victory but also a symbol of North Vietnam's ability to confront a technologically superior adversary. Coc subsequently participated in the training of new Vietnam Air Force pilots, sharing his knowledge and tactics with the generations that followed him.

Nguyen Van Coc is remembered as one of North Vietnam's greatest aviation aces and as a national hero who defended his country from the skies. His ability to confront cutting-edge U.S. technology and score significant victories in aerial combat positions him as a legendary figure in Vietnamese military aviation.

2. Charles B. DeBellevue: U.S. Air Force Flying Ace

Born August 15, 1945, in New Orleans, Louisiana, Charles Barbin DeBellevue was one of the most accomplished flying aces of the Vietnam War and the last United States Air Force pilot to earn the distinction of "Ace" in aerial combat. With 6 confirmed combat victories, DeBellevue is recognized not only as one of the most effective fighter pilots in Vietnam but also as the only Weapons Systems Officer (WSO) to achieve ace status during the conflict, achieving his victories from the back seat of an F-4 Phantom II.

After graduating from the University of Southwestern Louisiana (now the University of Louisiana at Lafayette) in 1968, DeBellevue entered the Air Force and became a Weapons Systems Officer. During his training, he showed an exceptional aptitude for aerial combat and was assigned to the 555th Tactical Fighter Squadron, also known as the "Triple Nickel," in Thailand, from where he flew missions over North Vietnam.

The F-4 Phantom II, the aircraft in which DeBellevue flew as a weapons officer, was a high-powered fighter used by American forces. Although it did not have an internal cannon, it was equipped with AIM-7 Sparrow and AIM-9 Sidewinder air-to-air missiles, both of which became DeBellevue's primary tools in his engagements. In the role of WSO, DeBellevue worked closely with the pilot to perform complex maneuvers and precise attack strategies.

On May 10, 1972, DeBellevue and his squadron pilot, Captain Steve Ritchie, scored their first two victories against enemy MiG-21s during a mission over North Vietnam. Later, July 8, Ritchie and DeBellevue shot down another MiG-21. By August, DeBellevue began flying with Captain John Madden, and together they scored three additional victories. On August 28, 1972, they managed to shoot down two more MiG-21s, cementing DeBellevue as the first Air Force air combat ace of the Vietnam War with a total of six kills.

These victories were strategically significant, as North Vietnamese MiG-21s posed a major threat to American bombing missions, and DeBellevue's skill in coordinating attacks and guiding missiles allowed his squadrons to outmaneuver the well-trained North Vietnamese air force.

For his bravery and success in combat, DeBellevue was awarded the Air Force Cross, the Silver Star, and the Distinguished Flying Medal, among other honors. His skill in battle and ability to collaborate effectively from his role as a WSO transformed his career into an example of professionalism and military prowess.

After the Vietnam War, DeBellevue continued his service in the Air Force, rising through the years to the rank of colonel. He played a crucial role in training pilots and weapons systems officers, helping to train new generations of airmen in combat and weapons systems operations. He retired in 1998 after 30 years of service.

3. Jeffrey S. Feinstein: The Last U.S. Air Force Ace

Jeffrey S. Feinstein, born January 29, 1945, in Chicago, Illinois, is one of the last U.S. fighter aces and the only Jewish weapons systems officer (WSO) to receive the "ace" distinction during the Vietnam War. With five confirmed victories, Feinstein achieved this historic status from the back seat of an F-4 Phantom II, serving as a weapons systems officer, the same role as his colleague Charles DeBellevue, who was also an Ace in Vietnam.

Feinstein joined the Air Force in 1968 after completing his undergraduate studies at the United States Air Force Academy. Initially, he was deemed ineligible for air service due to vision problems, but after eye surgery, he managed to overcome this obstacle and joined the air branch as a weapons systems officer. His determination and skill led to his assignment to the 13th Tactical Fighter Squadron, a unit within the 432nd Tactical Reconnaissance Wing at Udorn Air Force Base in Thailand.

Feinstein was sent to Vietnam at a time when the war was escalating into its dogfight phase, and American aircraft had to contend with a well-organized North Vietnamese air defense. The MiG-21, flown by experienced North Vietnamese airmen, was a highly maneuverable fighter that posed a significant threat to American missions. To meet this challenge, weapons systems officers on the F-4 Phantom II like Feinstein had to be exceptionally trained in the use of air-to-air missiles and in coordinating the aircraft's maneuvers with the pilot.

On October 31, 1972, Feinstein scored his fifth confirmed victory, thereby attaining ace status. Working closely with his pilot, Captain Ronald "Moses" Frazier, Feinstein demonstrated exceptional prowess in the use of AIM-7 Sparrow and AIM-9 Sidewinder air-to-air missiles, scoring a final kill that would cement his place in American aviation history. His meticulous approach, tactical skill, and missile guidance prowess in combat translated into a series of victories that earned him not only a place in the Aviation Hall of Fame but also many military decorations.

Feinstein's honors include the Distinguished Flying Cross and the Distinguished Flying Medal, in recognition of his bravery and success in combat. His status as an ace in an unconventional role for the time—weapons systems officer—underscored the importance of teamwork and collaboration in aerial combat.

After the war, Feinstein continued his service in the Air Force, where he was promoted to lieutenant colonel before retiring. Following his retirement, Feinstein devoted himself to academic and entrepreneurial pursuits, always maintaining a connection with Vietnam veterans and participating in events that commemorated the accomplishments of the era's pilots. Their legacy remains a testament to the skill and courage required in aerial combat, as well as the importance of each member of a fighter aircraft crew.

The Role of Combat Aviation from the End of the Vietnam War to Today

Since the end of the Vietnam War in 1975, combat aviation has evolved significantly, becoming a key tool for air superiority, surveillance, and global power projection. During this period, technological advancement has been constant, from the adoption of fourth- and fifth-generation fighters to the development of combat drones and smart missiles. Modern military aviation has not only changed the way we fight in the air but has also profoundly impacted tactics and strategies in land and maritime conflicts.

During the final years of the Cold War, the major players—the United States and the Soviet Union—competed in an arms race in which fourth-generation fighters, such as the F-15 Eagle and MiG-29, became symbols of air power. These aircraft, developed with superior maneuverability capabilities and longer combat range, demonstrated the importance of combining speed, firepower, and advanced technology on the air battlefield.

In the 1980s, the introduction of aircraft such as the F-16 Fighting Falcon and Su-27 consolidated the role of combat aviation in defense and preemptive attack. Fourth-generation fighters were designed with better flight control systems and more precise weapons, which increased lethality in air combat. During Operation Desert Storm in 1991, these aircraft proved essential to the rapid achievement of air superiority in Iraq, quickly destroying defenses and limiting the ability of the adversary to respond.

The 2000s marked the introduction of fifth-generation aviation, characterized using stealth technology, advanced sensor systems, and data fusion. Aircraft such as the US F-22 Raptor and F-35 Lightning II redefined the concept of air by being nearly undetectable by radar and possessing a superior ability to collect and share data in real time. These aircraft can operate in hostile environments undetected, offering a considerable tactical advantage and an increase in the ability to execute intelligence, surveillance, and reconnaissance (ISR) missions.

Fifth-generation aviation not only involves improvements in flight performance but is also deeply integrated into combat network systems, allowing pilots to receive real-time information and coordinate attacks more effectively. This capability has changed the dynamics of joint operations, allowing greater synchronization with units on land, sea, and in space.

Since the beginning of the 21st century, unmanned aerial vehicles (UAVs) have taken on a pivotal role in military operations. Drones such as the MQ-1 Predator and MQ-9 Reaper have been widely used in surveillance and precision strike missions. These drones offer a significant advantage: they can conduct extended missions without risking the life of a human pilot, making them ideal for operations in high-risk environments or for attacking specific targets with surgical precision.

The addition of drones to the military arsenal has enabled cost reductions and improved the ability of armed forces to monitor and respond quickly to emerging threats. As drone technology has advanced, the development of autonomous UAVs and artificial intelligence systems has opened new possibilities for the future of combat aviation.

The role of combat aviation has expanded with the growing importance of electronic and cyber warfare. Modern combat systems are designed to intercept, jam, and manipulate electronic signals, making it possible to interfere with enemy radar and communication systems. Aircraft such as the U.S. Navy's EA-18G Growler have been instrumental in electronic warfare, supporting air and ground forces in recent operations.

In addition, modern aviation systems are increasingly integrated into digital networks, allowing for greater synchronization between different military branches and allied nations. However, this interconnectedness has also brought vulnerabilities, and cybersecurity has become a priority in aircraft design and air operations.

The future of combat aviation points to greater automation and the use of artificial intelligence. Programs such as the U.S. Air Force's Skyborg are developing unmanned "companion aircraft" that can fly alongside manned fighters, assisting in reconnaissance, combat, and attack tasks. These "loyal companions" will offer new tactical options and reduce the risk to pilots on dangerous missions.

In addition, the development of sixth-generation fighters, expected to enter service in the next decade, includes advanced camouflage technologies, integrated artificial intelligence, hypersonic systems, and advanced electronic warfare capabilities. These aircraft will be capable of performing missions in increasingly complex environments, adapting in real-time to threats on the battlefield.

Since the end of the Vietnam War, combat aviation has evolved to meet the challenges of an ever-changing world, where technology and precision are essential. The combination of stealth aircraft, combat drones, and artificial intelligence technology has redefined the role of military aviation, preparing it for the demands of a modern war environment in which speed, adaptability, and precision are essential for success in combat; although, perhaps, the end of the flying aces... or perhaps, not.

The last beams of modern aviation:

1. Giora Epstein: The Israeli Flying Ace and the Greatest Ace of the Jet Age

Giora Epstein, also known as Giora Even after changing his last name, is the most victorious fighter pilot of jet age, having scored 17 confirmed kills throughout his career. Born on May 20, 1938, in Nes Ziona, Israel, Epstein is considered one of the greatest flying aces and one of the most admired for his ability to take on multiple enemies, particularly during the Middle East conflicts of the 1960s and 1970s.

Epstein joined the Israeli Air Force (IAF) in 1956 but was initially rejected for pilot training due to a heart condition. However, his determination led him to serve as a paratrooper before finally being accepted into flight school in 1961. Once trained, he quickly demonstrated his skill as an aviator, and his precision and agility in combat marked him as an exceptional pilot.

Epstein's combat career began in the Six-Day War in 1967, although he scored no kills in this conflict. However, it was during the War of Attrition (1967-1970) and the Yom Kippur War (1973) that Epstein proved himself to be a fearsome pilot in the air.

Equipped with French Mirage III fighters and later the IAI Nesher, an improved version of the Mirage, Epstein racked up most of his victories during the Yom Kippur War. His skills allowed him to skillfully shoot down enemy pilots in high-stakes situations and one-on-many engagements. On one occasion, Epstein shot down four MiG-21s in a single day, demonstrating exceptional visual acuity that allowed him to see and react to threats before his adversaries.

Epstein was a master of complex aerial maneuvers, and his knowledge of the Mirage and Nesher gave him a considerable advantage in combat. His precision with air-to-air missiles and his expertise in close combat (dogfighting) made him a legend. Unlike many other aces, Epstein preferred to engage enemy MiG fighters at close range, where he could fully exploit his aircraft's maneuverability.

Of Epstein's 17 victories, the majority were against MiG-21s and MiG-17s flown by Arab pilots during the Yom Kippur War engagements. These victories not only contributed to Israel's air superiority during the conflict but also earned him respect and recognition in the Israeli Air Force and the aviation world.

After his retirement in 1997, Epstein remained an inspirational figure within military aviation. His record of 17 jet combat victories places him as the most successful jet ace in history, an achievement that few have matched or surpassed in the modern era. Epstein was awarded multiple honors, including the Israeli Distinguished Service Medal, for his contributions and combat prowess.

Giora Epstein's legacy lives on in the IAF and in the history of military aviation, where his bravery and skill continue to inspire pilots around the world. His ability to overcome superior forces and ability to remain focused under fire make him an aviation legend, whose combat techniques and focus are still studied in military academies.

2. Yiftah Spector: Israeli flying ace and key figure in the Israeli Air Force

Yiftah Spector is one of the most prominent fighter pilots in the history of the Israeli Air Force (IAF), known for his combat skills, leadership, and contributions to Israeli military aviation. Spector amassed 15 confirmed victories throughout his career, primarily in conflicts such as the Six-Day War (1967), the Yom Kippur War

(1973), and the Lebanon War (1982). He is also known for having been one of the pilots on the famous 1981 mission that destroyed the Osirak nuclear reactor in Iraq, considered one of the most significant air raids in Israel's history.

Yiftah Spector was born on October 20, 1940, in Israel, to a pioneering family in the country. His interest in aviation began at an early age, and from a young age, he showed exceptional flying skills. He joined the Israeli Air Force in 1958 and completed his pilot training, quickly standing out for his quick reflexes and mastery of combat aircraft.

Spector's career unfolded during a period of intense conflict for Israel, allowing him to gain real combat experience at a young age. He took part in the Six-Day War in 1967, when Israel launched preemptive strikes against the air forces of Egypt, Syria, and Jordan. During this conflict, he demonstrated outstanding performance by shooting down several enemy aircraft and quickly established himself as one of the IAF's elite pilots.

In 1973, during the Yom Kippur War, Spector played a crucial role in Israel's air defense efforts against Egypt and Syria, achieving further kills and displaying exceptional leadership in times of high pressure. In this conflict, the Israeli air forces faced opponents with advanced equipment supplied by the Soviet Union, making each mission a major challenge. Despite this, Spector racked several more victories and cemented his reputation as a highly effective and strategic pilot in combat.

One of the most significant moments in Spector's career was his participation in Operation Opera, the 1981 mission in which the IAF bombed and destroyed the Osirak nuclear reactor in Iraq. This mission was seen as a preventative measure to prevent Iraq from developing nuclear weapons that could pose a threat to Israel. Spector was one of the pilots who flew the F-16 during the mission, carrying out the operation with surgical precision and contributing to the success of an attack that was considered highly risky and technically challenging.

Operation Opera was a milestone in Israel's military history and an example of the IAF's ability to successfully carry out complex missions. Spector's participation in this mission further elevated his status as one of the Air Force's most respected pilots.

Throughout his career, Yiftah Spector received numerous accolades for his bravery, combat skills, and leadership. His record of victories, coupled with his participation in key strategic missions, cemented him as one of the IAF's most recognizable aces. He eventually retired from the IAF with the rank of colonel, leaving behind a legacy of professionalism and commitment to Israel's defense.

After his retirement, Yiftah Spector remained active in Israeli public life and took a critical stance in some respects. In 2003, he was one of the IAF pilots who signed a letter expressing their opposition to bombing raids in Palestinian civilian areas, arguing ethical and moral issues surrounding IAF operations. This stance sparked controversy and was met with criticism, but it also showed his sense of ethical responsibility, which added a unique dimension to his figure as a military pilot.

Yiftah Spector remains a relevant figure in the history of Israeli aviation. His bravery and skills as a fighter pilot, along with his participation in critical missions and his ethical stance in civilian life, have made him an icon of military and moral commitment. His legacy inspires new generations of IAF pilots and his name is synonymous with excellence and bravery in the world of military aviation.

3. Majid Zugbi: Arab Air Ace

Majid Zugbi is remembered as one of the most skilled pilots in the Syrian Air Force during the 1960s and 1970s, a period marked by intense conflicts between Arab forces and Israel. Although he is not as well known internationally, his bravery and combat achievements established him as a hero in Syria and other Arab countries.

Majid Zugbi was born in Syria, at a time when aviation was beginning to gain importance in the military field in the Middle East. In his early years, he showed great interest and exceptional skills in handling aircraft, which led him to join the Syrian Air Force, where he quickly stood out among his peers. His intensive training in Soviet aircraft allowed him to become familiar with MIGs, key models in Syrian air combat at the time.

Zugbi's career coincided with a period of great tension in the region, especially due to the Arab-Israeli conflicts. Syria and its Arab allies faced Israel on several occasions, and Zugbi participated in several engagements in which aerial and tactical skills were decisive.

Zugbi was assigned to fly the MiG-21, a Soviet-designed fighter jet that became the backbone of the Arab air forces during the Six-Day War in 1967 and later in the War of Attrition and the Yom Kippur War in 1973. In these conflicts, he is credited with several aerial victories against Israeli fighters, facing an air force that was equipped with technologically superior aircraft, such as the Mirage III and the F-4 Phantom.

The Yom Kippur War was one of the major flashpoints in the Arab-Israeli conflict, and it was also the contest that most contributed to Zugbi's reputation as a skilled and daring pilot. During this war, Syria launched air and ground attacks to retake territory lost in the previous conflict. Known for his combat prowess and ability to execute evasive maneuvers, Zugbi flew numerous missions defending Syrian airspace and engaging directly with Israeli pilots, managing to survive and score victories despite the technological disadvantage.

Although detailed official records of all Zugbi's missions are not available, his career made him a symbol of resistance in Syria. His combat achievements earned him the respect of his countrymen and other Arab countries who saw him as a hero of the Arab cause.

After the war, Majid Zugbi continued to serve in the Syrian Air Force for a few years before retiring. His legacy as a Syrian flying ace has remained in Syria's military history and in the memories of those who saw him fly with bravery and skill during the difficult conflicts in the region.

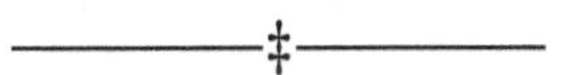

Other books by the author Phillips Tahuer that you will find on this platform:

- The greatest conspiracy theories

- Great robberies in history

- Famous murderers - the evil side of the mind-

- Lives in captivity - Stories of real kidnappings-

- Agents, informants and traitors - the world of espionage-

- Pirates of the 21st century

- Tragic love

- 30 curiosities of World War II

- Dark experiments on humans

- Real-life heroes

- Powerful men in modern history

- Valentine's Day stories

- Lessons in practical psychology

- Deserters

- Attacks and assassinations